Mai-Lan Q.D. Bell

A
Transformation
from
GOD

"But those who drink the water I give will never be
thirsty again. It becomes a fresh, bubbling spring
within them, giving them eternal life."
—John 4:14 (NLT)

Entegrity Choice Publishing
PO Box 453
Powder Springs, GA 30127
info@entegritypublishing.com

The views expressed in this work are solely those of the author and do not necessarily reflect the views of the publisher, and the publisher hereby disclaims any responsibility for them.

Book Cover Designed by Kylie Kroukamp

ISBN: 979-8-9850792-5-8

Library of Congress Control Number: 2023901261

Printed in the United States of America

Dedication

I dedicate this book to my Heavenly Father
God and His Son Jesus Christ.

Foreword

It is an honor and privilege to write this fore-word for Mai-Lan Bell. We shared the same neighborhood since elementary school and at-tended the same high school. Our mothers were Spelman College sisters in the same class, and we ended up being sisters in Christ attending the same church.

Although, as young adults, Mai-Lan and I moved to distant locations and followed our own distinct journeys, after I returned to Atlanta in 2007, our paths began to merge once again.

She is truly a sincere woman of God with a passion for what God has called her to do, that is, working with single moms like she was.

This book expresses evidence of her heart-felt urgency to advise, not only single moms but all of us, how to live an abundant life no matter what we are going through.

I urge everyone to read this book and allow God and the Holy Spirit to minister to you concerning whatever you are going through. "God is no respecter of persons" (Acts 10:34). He certainly revealed things to me as I read this book, and He will do the same for you.

I want to thank Mai-Lan for this precious opportunity. I know she has committed this work to the Lord, and He will bring her success. "Commit your works to the Lord [submit and trust Him], And your plans will succeed [if you respond to His will and guidance]" (Proverbs 16:3).

Soli Deo Gloria
(To God Alone Be the Glory)
Marilyn Mitchell-Chapman, DDS
MA in Christian Education
Apologetics, BS major Zoology/minor
Chemistry

Acknowledgment

To God be the Glory for the things that He has done, is doing, and will do in my life. Everything that I am and hope to be, I owe it all to God and His Son Jesus Christ, who is without a doubt the author and finisher of my faith. I thank You God for sending your Son Jesus to die on the cross so I didn't have to, and for raising Your Son Jesus up from the dead who is alive today.

Thank you, God, for sending Your Holy Spirit to guide me in all truth, and for loving me unconditionally! Thank you, God, for blessing me with my two most precious gifts from You, my children James Denzil and Michael Lennox, whom You used as the inspiration for my transformation.

Table of Contents

Introduction

At an early age, I accepted Jesus Christ as my Lord and Savior. Somewhere along the way, however, I strayed from God, formed my own beliefs about life, and did as I pleased. Nevertheless, I never stopped believing that God was with me.

One day, as I was standing in the family room at home, I suddenly heard God's voice clearly saying to me, "You are my witness!" I don't remember what I was actually doing prior to this that led to me hearing God's voice tell me this, but I do know it was real. Witness is defined as follows: to testify, to tell what you have seen or experienced. A Christian is to be a witness by sharing personal experiences of what Jesus has done in and for them.

At the age of twenty-seven, I gave birth to my first child. I was a single mother. A single mother is any female who has a child or children and is not legally married. She may be divorced, widowed, or never married; she may be living with a boyfriend or even engaged to be married. When my first child was almost two months old, as his dad and I were in love, we got married. Three years later, during my third month of pregnancy with our second child, my husband and I separated.

I moved back home with my parents and maternal grandparents, and remained separated from my husband for several years. My own parents had been married for forty-one years at the time of my mom's passing, my maternal grandparents for over sixty years, and, prior to my father-in-law's passing, my husband's parents were similarly married for many long years. Naturally, I thought that my husband and I would be married for many long years, but . . . divorce happened! I was a single mother once again; this time with two young children.

Living at home with my parents and grand-parents, I had a strong and trustworthy support system, with the bonus of live-in babysitters! On the one hand, this meant I didn't have to worry about anyone harming my children. When I went out, I knew my children were safe and loved. On the other hand, this arrangement was way too comfortable and way too convenient, because it allowed me the freedom to revert back to the "single" lifestyle I had enjoyed before having children. Then one night, God stepped in. That was the beginning of me becoming a witness for Christ!

It is through sharing our testimonies that we help others to see how good God is and how much He loves us. At the end of each chapter, there is an opportunity for you to self-reflect by answering questions relevant to the chapter's contents. There is also a suggested scripture reading for you to spend quiet time with God, with space provided for notetaking. It is my prayer that this book will be a blessing to all who read it.

1

A Divine Encounter

*"Here I am! I stand at the door and knock.
If anyone hears my voice and opens the
door, I will come in and eat with that
person, and they with me."
—Revelation 3:20 (NIV)*

I had fallen asleep on the sofa while watching television in the basement. Suddenly, I was awakened by a knock at the window. I got up and looked out of the window, but no one was there. I returned to the sofa and continued watching television, and of course, the television ended up watching me. I had fallen asleep again. Several hours later, at exactly 4:44 a.m., I was awakened by a gentle touch on my shoulder; but once again, no one was there. This time, I turned the television off and went to bed.

After a few hours of sleep, I woke up saying the words, "If ye have faith as a grain of mustard seed." Having attended a Bible-based school during the first seven years of my schooling and attended church as a child, and with a mother and grandmother who talked to me about God, the foundation of being able to recognize God's voice had been laid out for me.

Recognizing these words to be that of a scripture, I got up and grabbed my Bible from my dresser. I looked in the back of it, in the concordance, and found the scripture in Matthew 17:20 (KJV). Sitting on the side of the bed, I began reading.

"And Jesus said unto them. Because of your unbelief: for verily I say unto you, if ye have faith as a grain of mustard seed, ye shall say unto this mountain, Remove hence to yonder place; and it shall remove; and nothing shall be impossible unto you."

A mustard seed is about 1–2 millimeters in diameter; it is small enough to fit between my thumb and index finger, where it cannot even be seen.

Why did I wake up quoting words from this scripture? What was God trying to tell me? I always thought I had faith; was God saying that I didn't? These were some of the thoughts racing through my mind.

I read this scripture over and over, trying to understand just what God was saying to me. I knew that in time, God would eventually reveal to me the "why." I let it go and went on with my day, thinking nothing more about it. But that wasn't the end of it. Afterwards, for the next few weeks, every morning, I would wake up quoting some words from a scripture, some of which I was familiar with and some I was not. Each time, like the first time, I would get my Bible and look in the concordance as to where I could find the particular scripture I had been quoting. Eventually, I ceased to quote scripture upon awaking, but my desire to read the Bible had increased. God was drawing me closer to Him.

Finally, God revealed to me the "why" concerning the scripture in Mathew 17:20, which I first woke up quoting words from. It wasn't that I didn't have faith, but rather, God wanted me to increase my faith through reading His word more.

*"So then faith comes by hearing and
hearing from the word of God."*
—Romans 10:17 (NKJV)

One day, while reading Revelation 3:20, I was reminded of the knock at the window that woke me up that first night, when I had fallen asleep in the basement and felt the gentle touch on my shoulder that caused me to finally get up and go to my bed.

*"Here I am! I stand at the door and knock.
If anyone hears my voice and opens the door
I will come in and eat with that person,
and they with me."*

Waking up quoting words from scriptures, I heard God's voice. Opening my Bible to find the scriptures, I opened the door to God. He came in, eating with me, feeding me His word. Allowing God through His word to transform me, I ate with Him!

My Prayer

Gracious and Loving Father, thank You God for getting my attention, and for Your word, which is a lamp to my feet and a light for my path. Thank You God for being my everlasting light.
In Jesus name I pray, Amen.

SELF-REFLECTION

How has God tried to get my attention?

How often do I spend time with God reading His word?

FOR PARENTS

What kind of foundation have I laid down for my child or children in helping them to recognize God's call in their life?

QUIET TIME WITH GOD

Suggested scripture reading: **John 10:27–28**

What is God saying to me in this scripture?

_____

_____

2

A God Dream

*"God does speak—sometimes one way
and sometimes another—even though people
may not understand it. He speaks in a dream
or vision of the night when people are in a deep
sleep, lying on their beds. He speaks in their ears
and frightens them with warnings to turn them
away from doing wrong and to keep them from
being proud. God does this to save people from
death, to keep them from dying."
—Job 33:14–18 (NCV)*

There was music playing. Women were dressed in low-cut, short, tight-fitting dresses, and people were dancing in a smoky room. On the tables, there were glasses filled with bottles of beer and other alcoholic beverages, and packs of cigarettes with a big red slash on each. In my ear, I heard a soft and gentle voice saying to me, "Stop smoking." Although this was a dream, it was also my reality! Hanging out in clubs and at late-night parties, wearing low-cut short tight-fitting dresses, drinking alcohol, and smoking cigarettes was my lifestyle. I enjoyed this lifestyle, to the extent that I felt I couldn't have a good time without smoking and drinking. It was also a lifestyle that, in my dream, God was revealing to me needed to change. I was on a road to destruction, and I didn't even know it.

For almost twenty years, I was addicted to cigarettes; sometimes, I would smoke almost two and a half packs a day. Then one day, as I stood in the garage at home and lit a cigarette, my children walked in. Although my smoking was no secret to them, a strange feeling came over me, and smoking in front of them suddenly didn't feel right. I began to think to myself, "What kind of example am I setting for my children to not smoke cigarettes if I smoke cigarettes?" Soon after, during my quiet time with God, I read 1 Corinthians 6:19–20 (AMP): "Do you not know that your body is a temple of the Holy Spirit who is within you, whom you have [received as a gift] from God, and that you are not your own [property]? You were bought with a price [you were actually purchased with the precious blood of Jesus and made His own]. So then, honor and glorify God with your body."

Reading this scripture, I couldn't help but think of God's love for me, and of Him sacrificing His Only Son Jesus for me. I thought about the strange feeling that had come over me when my children walked in as I was about to light the cigarette. I now know that this was not just a strange feeling or a random thought but rather the Holy Spirit, whom I received from God.

I realized that I needed to lay a good foundation for my children, like that which had been laid down for me as a little girl. My children needed to see me honoring God with my body so that they could learn how to honor God with their own bodies. By filling my body, God's temple, with nicotine, I was not honoring God with my body; similarly, by filling it with alcohol to the point of intoxication (and even, on one occasion, to the point of getting a DUI and consequently spending a few minutes behind bars), I was definitely not honoring God with my body.

> *"Don't be drunk with wine,*
> *because it will ruin your life.*
> *Instead be filled with the Holy Spirit."*
> *—Ephesians 5:18*

When it came to the way I dressed, according to 1 Timothy 2:9–10 (KJV), I was not dressing like the Christian woman I professed to be, nor was I setting a good example as a mother for my children.

"I also want the women to dress modestly, with decency and propriety, adorning themselves, not with elaborate hairstyles or gold or pearls or expensive clothes,¹⁰ but with good deeds, appropriate for women who profess to worship God."

The dream was real: my lifestyle needed to change. I initially tried achieving this on my own. Instead of smoking cigarettes, I switched over to smoking cigarillos thinking that was better; it wasn't. I was still putting nicotine in my body. Smoking back and forth between cigarettes and cigarillos I was desperate to change, not only for my children's sake but also to honor God with my body. Knowing that it was His will for me to do so, I prayed, asking God to deliver me from my harmful lifestyle.

"This is the confidence we have in approaching God: that if we ask anything according to his will, he hears us. And if we know that he hears us—whatever we ask—we know that we have what we asked of him."
—*1 John 5:14–15 (NIV)*

In 1994, God delivered me from smoking cigarettes, cigarillos, drinking alcohol, and even wearing short low-cut tight-fitting dresses and low-cut shirts. God also delivered me from hanging out in clubs and attending late-night parties. This was the beginning of God transforming my life!

"I advise you to obey only the Holy Spirit's instructions. He will tell you where to go and what to do, and then you won't always be doing the wrong things your evil nature wants you to."
—*Galatians 5:16 (TLB)*

My Prayer

Heavenly Father, thank You for delivering me from an unhealthy and destructive lifestyle, and for showing me how to honor You God with my body, so that I can enjoy good health and set an example of good lifestyle choices for others. Keep me on the right path, Lord God. In the name of Your Son Jesus, I pray, Amen.

SELF-REFLECTION

What lifestyle changes do I need to be making in my life?

How am I honoring God with my body and the clothes that I wear?

FOR PARENTS

Am I honoring God in my role as a parent by the lifestyle that I am living for my child or children?

QUIET TIME WITH GOD

Suggested scripture reading: **1 Corinthians 10:31**

What is God saying to me in this scripture?

_____

_____

3

Dirty Language
and Dirty Behavior Actions

*"But now is the time to cast off and
throw away all these rotten garments of anger,
hatred, cursing, and dirty language."*
—Colossians 3:8 (TLB)

When I first read the above scripture, my eyes immediately focused on the word "cursing," and I remember thinking to myself, "When did profanity become a such a part of the everyday English language?" As a young child, I never heard profanity used on TV or in song lyrics, and for the most part, females definitely didn't use profanity. If a man used profanity in the presence of a female, he would immediately apologize for his language. I don't ever recall hearing my mother or grandmother using any profanity. As they were my role models, I didn't use profanity either; well, at least for the most part.

In the early 1970s, when I was in high school,

I tried using profanity to "fit in," so to speak. A very close friend at the time told me that I did not know how to curse (I really didn't know there was a certain way to curse!). She continued to share with me that it didn't sound right coming from my mouth, and told me, "You should just stop trying to curse because it doesn't fit you." And so, I took her advice! Looking at this scripture again, I realized that although I didn't have a rotten garment of cursing, I was carrying around rotten garments of anger, hatred, and even dirty language, just not spoken out loud.

Later, I had candy molds for just about anything you could imagine, including X-rated ones. I would make dark chocolate, milk chocolate, and white chocolate candies in candy molds of the male and female anatomy! I baked cakes and decorated them with whatever part of the anatomy one desired, or sold them separately for people to enjoy as candy only.

I actually had a nice little business going there for a while, with quite a few regular customers.

Then one day, I read Isaiah 43:7 (TLB), "All who claim me as their God will come, for I have made them for my glory; I created them." God is my creator, and I definitely claim Him as my

God; I was created to bring glory to His name. However, after reading this scripture I realized that I wasn't bringing glory to God by making X-rated candies. God had not given me this talent to create this kind of candy, which was causing others to lust over my edibles and talk dirty to each other; so I repented. When some of my customers learned that I was no longer making these types of candies, a few asked me if they could buy the molds from me; some were even willing to pay me good money for them. Thinking about it, the Holy Spirit reminded me of the scripture in 1 Timothy 6:10 (NKJV), "For the love of money is a root of all kinds of evil, for which some have strayed from the faith in their greediness, and pierced themselves through with many sorrows."

I threw the X-rated molds away and vowed to God to not ever make those type of candies again! Had I sold the molds to someone else, then I would have been contributing to them perpetuating the behavior for which I had repented.

"Let each of you look out not only for his own interests, but also for the interests of others."
—Philippians 2:4 (NKJV)

My Prayer

Gracious and Loving God,
thank You God for creating me for Your glory.
Help me Lord God to always bring glory
to Your Holy name in all that I do.
In Jesus name I pray, Amen.

SELF-REFLECTION

What rotten garments do I need to throw away?

What talents has God given me, and how am I using my talents to bring glory to God?

FOR PARENTS

How am I encouraging my child or children to use their talents for God's glory?

QUIET TIME WITH GOD

Suggested scripture reading: **1 Peter 4:10–13**

What is God saying to me in this scripture?

_____

_____

4

Learning to Forgive

*"Let all bitterness, wrath, anger, clamor, and evil
speaking be put away from you, with all malice.
And be kind to one another, tenderhearted,
forgiving one another,
even as God in Christ forgave you."*
—Ephesians 4:31–32 (NKJV)

When my children were in middle school, my youngest son played basketball. One afternoon, during halftime at one of his games, a friend of mine, who was also a parent with a son playing basketball, began sharing with me something she was reading in an article on racial issues. While recounting the article, she said to me, "My children know not to bring home a date who is not their color." I was shocked by her comment to say the least, especially because she's a Christian!

The Bible clearly tells us in Genesis 5:2 (NLT), "He created them male and female, and he blessed them and called them 'human.'" Some translations say "mankind," which is defined as "human race." God didn't say he created a black male and a black female, or a white male and a white female, but rather, He created them male and female. God doesn't look at the color of our skin because he created all of us. As Christians, we are to be imitators of God, loving all people.

> *"Therefore, be imitators of God as dear children. And walk in love, as Christ also has loved us and given Himself for us, an offering and a sacrifice to God for a sweet-smelling aroma."*
> *—Ephesians 5:1–2 (NKJV)*

I have been in three different abusive relationships in my life. My first abusive relationship happened when I was away in college. It began when my boyfriend at the time asked me to do a particular sexual act, and I refused. He put a gun to my head, and threatened to use it if I didn't. With tears streaming down my face, he removed the gun from my head. He hugged me tightly and apologized, saying he was sorry. He promised to never try to hurt me again. I forgave him. Sometime later during an argument, he hit me in the face so hard that for a moment all I could see were stars. And yes, I forgave him and we continued our relationship.

I don't know whether or not he would have eventually abused me again, because I later almost died from an almost ruptured appendix, and had to have emergency surgery. After having surgery and being released from the hospital, I returned home, and did not return to school or have any further contact with him. I never told my parents about the abuse I experienced with him.

I was not strong enough to leave him on my own. Having to have emergency surgery allowed me the opportunity to finally leave him for good! I thank God for the surgery I had to have.

*"Give thanks in all circumstances; for this
is God's will for you in Christ Jesus."*
—1 Corinthians 5:18

My second encounter with abuse happened with my first husband, I was twenty-three years old. He had been drinking heavily the night before, showing signs of possibly being abusive. I left and went to my parent's home to spend the night. The next day, I returned home to talk to him to see about us going to counseling, especially for his drinking problem. I felt threatened, so my mother went with me. I thought having my mother there with me, he would not try to hurt me. That did not stop him from doing the inevitable. In the midst of our conversation, and in my mother's presence, he hit me so hard in my face, I thought he had broken my nose. Thank God it wasn't broken. My mother and I left. When we got back to my parent's home, I immediately started looking through the phonebook (Yellow Pages) for an attorney. Finding an attorney, I called and set up an appointment to file for a divorce. I was not going to give him a second chance to hit me again, as I had done in my previous relationship.

Later that night my husband came to my parent's home, and made a scene outside. He was intoxicated. The police were called, and his car was towed, and he was taken into custody. When he finally got home having been sobered up and released, he called me. We had a long talk. He apologized for everything, and of course I forgave him. The next day before I could go to the appointment with the attorney, I received a phone call from his cousin saying that my husband had committed suicide.

When my third and final abusive relationship happened, I had no more forgiveness in my heart. Instead, I held a grudge. As my friend continued talking about the article, I could hear in her voice the hatred she had been harboring in her heart of how some people have treated others in the past. Our conversation sparked something in me: it reminded me of the feelings of hatred I was carrying in my own heart towards my last abuser. Though the reason was different from my friend's, based on her remarks, the hatred that I felt in my heart seemed to be the same kind of hatred as what my friend described that she was feeling. I was being a hypocrite. Who was I to judge my friend, when I too was guilty of holding a grudge against someone?

> *"Why do you look at the speck of sawdust in your brother's eye and pay no attention to the plank in your own eye? How can you say to your brother, 'Let me take the speck out of your eye,' when all the time there is a plank in your own eye? You hypocrite, first take the plank out of your own eye,*

and then you will see clearly to remove
the speck from your brother's eye."
—Matthew 7:3–5 (NIV)

"And when you stand praying if
you hold anything against anyone, forgive
them, so that your Father in heaven may
forgive you your sins."
—Mark 11:25 (NIV)

After reading those scriptures, I recall having a long talk with God. I just couldn't see how I could forgive someone who had hurt me the way this person had done.

"For all have sinned and fall
short of the glory of God."
—Romans 3:23 (NIV)

I knew that I had done some sinful things in my life, but it wasn't until I came across an on-line Ten Commandment Test that I realized that the Ten Commandments, God's laws, were created to help us take a look at ourselves.

*"Now do you see it? No one can
ever be made right in God's sight by doing
what the law commands. For the more we know
of God's laws, the clearer it becomes that we
aren't obeying them; his laws serve only to
make us see that we are sinners."*
—Romans 3:20 (TLB)

This Ten Commandment test helped me to see just how sinful my life really was. It was very clear to me that I not only needed God's forgiveness but also needed His help to forgive my last abuser. I prayed, acknowledging to God my forgiveness for this person. I thought this was the end of it, but it wasn't.

The church that I was a member of at the time was having a church picnic, and God led me to invite to the picnic this person. I remember thinking to myself, "Really, God?" Nevertheless, I did as God led me to do, but, in my heart, I was hoping that the person would not show up; however, he did. My heart was racing with anxiety when I saw him walk into the room. The memory of what he had done to me flashed before me. I took a deep breath and prayed a very short prayer for

God to give me the strength to forgive this person face to face. Immediately, God's peace that ". . . surpasses all understanding" (Philippians 4:7), kicked in and calmed me down.

I walked over to this person, greeted him, thanked him for coming, and asked if he would step to the side so I could speak to him privately. I said to him, "I wanted to let you know that I forgive you for what you did to me." His response was something I never expected. He said to me, "I wanted to ask for your forgiveness, but I didn't know how." For a moment, I was speechless. God was using this situation to help me better understand the scripture in Mark 11:25. This person was not holding a grudge against me; I had been the one holding a grudge against him. Forgiveness was for me. It was my responsibility to forgive this person, whether I had known them or not. Forgiveness is a must.

"And when you stand praying if you hold anything against anyone, forgive them, so that your Father in heaven may forgive you your sins."
—Mark 11:25 (NIV)

Later, while reading an article explaining how holding grudges can affect one's health, I couldn't help thinking of my mom. In 1998, my mom passed away due to colon cancer. I remember when her doctor told us there was nothing else they could do for her, and that he had never seen anything like this before. What he was referring to was how the cancer had eaten away at her stomach, which was evidenced by visible holes.

When my granddad (my mother's dad) died in 1996, as I read his obituary, which my mother had written, I realized that she was holding a grudge against him for a career-related decision that he had made. Unfortunately, at that time, I was unaware of the relationship between holding grudges and one's health. It wasn't until some years later that God revealed to me that what had happened to my mom was a result of the unforgiveness in her heart. Thus, I have witnessed firsthand the importance of forgiving others.

Because hatred is a learned behavior, as a parent, I realize the damage that I could have done to my children if I had continued setting an example of hatred in my heart by holding a grudge against someone. As a Christian, I would not have been setting a good example for my children.

> *"Anyone who says he is a Christian should live as Christ did. Dear brothers, I am not writing out a new rule for you to obey, for it is an old one you have always had, right from the start. You have heard it all before. Yet it is always new, and works for you just as it did for Christ; and as we obey this commandment, to love one another, the darkness in our lives disappears and the new light of life in Christ shines in. Anyone who says he is walking in the light of Christ but dislikes his fellow man is still in darkness. But whoever loves his fellow man is "walking in the light" and can see his way without stumbling around in darkness and sin."*
> *—1 John 2:6–10 (TLB)*

My Prayer

*Almighty and Sovereign God, thank You Father
for opening my eyes and helping me to see and
understand that just as You Lord God created
me, You also created the one that I was holding a
grudge against. Thank You God for delivering me
from a spirit of hatred, and for helping me to
be a better Christian. In the precious name of
Your Son Jesus I pray, Amen.*

SELF-REFLECTION

Who do I need to forgive?
*(Remember, it can be someone whose name you
do not even know, but something happened,
and you're holding a grudge against them.)*

FOR THOSE EXPERIENCING
ANY HEALTH ISSUES

Is it possible that my health issues are a result
of my holding a grudge toward someone or
something?

FOR PARENTS

Am I setting a good example for my child or children about what it means to be a Christian, or am I teaching them to hate?

QUIET TIME WITH GOD

Suggested scripture reading: **Luke 6:28**

What is God saying to me in this scripture?

The Ten Commandments Test may be found at this website: https://www.fbbc.com/messages/kohl_live_ten_commandments.htm.

5

Renewing the Mind

"Do not conform to the pattern of this world, but
be transformed by the renewing of your mind.
Then you will be able to test and approve what
God's will is—his good, pleasing and perfect will."
—Romans 12:2 (NIV)

As I sat and listened to the testimonies of young women who had contemplated having an abortion but didn't, I couldn't help thinking of a time when I believed that having an abortion was okay to do. I believed that it was a woman's right to choose what she wanted to do with her body: her body, her right. I was wrong!

Life begins at conception. When a child is conceived, they are a person, a precious innocent child, a living human being. That living human being inside its mother's womb is not the mother's body but rather the body of another human being.

"You made all the delicate inner parts
of my body and knit them together
in my mother's womb."
—*Psalm 139:13 (NLT)*

Womb is defined as follows: uterus, the site of an unborn baby's growth until birth. In other words, a mother's womb is the carrier for human life. When a woman has an abortion, the pregnancy is ended so that it does not result in the birth of a child. Abortion is defined as the deliberate termination of a human pregnancy. The word deliberate means that it is done consciously and intentionally. Murder is the legal term for the intentional killing of someone or the killing of someone as the result of a complete disregard for their life. One of the Ten Commandments in Exodus 20:13 reads, "Thou shalt not kill"; other translations say, "You shall not murder." But yet, before I had children, I did.

I remember sitting in the clinic before they called me back, hoping that my baby's daddy (my boyfriend at that time), who was there with me, would change his mind about me having an abortion and say, "Let's go," but he didn't. Waiting in silence, many thoughts were rushing through my head. Thoughts like, "I should just get up and leave, and call someone to pick me up." Then I thought about my parents. What would they say if they even knew I was pregnant? Would I have their support if I decided not to go through with the abortion? Would they still love me? Would they be so disappointed in me that they would want nothing to do with me or my baby? Finally, I was called to the examining room in preparation for the procedure.

Upon entering the room, I was asked, "Is this what you want?" Hesitantly, I allowed fear to control my response, and the procedure took place. Afterward, I spent many nights hearing a baby cry in my sleep, and many times, I myself would cry because of what I had done. This was an emotionally and mentally painful time in my life. I vowed to never again have another abortion, and I didn't! I thank God that I chose life. My way of thinking, that I had a right to have an abortion, was totally wrong. But this was not the only thing that I was wrong about.

I have always known that sex was created to be shared between a man and a woman, but I didn't always attach the marriage aspect to this. The scripture in Genesis 2:25 (NIV) says,

"Adam and his wife were both naked, and they felt no shame." When I first read this scripture, it did not register to me that the reason why Adam and his wife felt no shame for their nudity was because they were married to each other, and therefore, there was nothing for them to be ashamed about. Instead, I looked at this scripture as an example of intimacy between a man and a woman, rather than acknowledging the fact that they were husband and wife. I even remember my mother used to tell me that I should wait until marriage to have sex. At the time, I didn't realize that this was actually godly advice, and instead interpreted it as merely her opinion; as a result, I formed my own opinion and beliefs when I became an adult. I believed that having sex outside wedlock was acceptable as long as both parties were adults and the man and woman loved each other. After all, that is how I first became a single mom. When I became a single mom the second time around as a result of divorce, the Holy Spirit led me to gain a clearer understanding about God's will regarding sex. I suppose God did this because I had misunderstood the meaning of Genesis 2:25 and what my mother had told me. To clarify my understanding of God's will regarding sex, I had to seek the one who created sex: God Himself!

I found my answer in 1 Thessalonians 4:3, plain as day: "For this is the will of God, even your sanctification, that ye should abstain from fornication." The word "abstain" means to refrain from something by one's own choice. Fornication refers to voluntary or consensual sexual intercourse between two people who are not married to each other. As I continued reading the chapter, I began to realize how wrong my way of thinking about sex had been. I was reminded not only of what my mom had told me but also of a time when I had spoken to a friend who had come to me for advice about taking her relationship with her boyfriend at the time to the next level of physical intimacy. My advice to her was that as long as she and her boyfriend loved each other and used protection, having sex was okay, if that was what they both wanted to do. That was definitely not godly advice. Had I known God's word as I do now, my advice would have been much different in helping her to make a godly choice. Thank God for His grace!

Having chosen life and learned God's truth regarding sex, my mind was renewed. I wanted to change and do things according to God's will, in both my actions and my advice to others. I remember crying out to God with remorse in a way that I had never done before, and even praying in a way that I had never prayed before. I asked God to forgive me, not only for my actions but also for having given ungodly advice to others and thus caused them to stray away from Him.

God is faithful. God forgave me.

"If we confess our sins, he is faithful and just to forgive us our sins and cleanse us from all unrighteousness."
—1 John 1:9 (NKJV)

My Prayer

Heavenly Father, thank You God for helping me to understand why abortion is wrong, and for forgiving me from the act of abortion. Thank You God for helping me to understand that it is Your will that sex be shared between a man and woman as husband and wife in the marriage relationship only. Thank you, God, for forgiving me for having sex outside of the marriage relationship. Thank You God for forgiving me for giving the wrong advice to others in the past where sex was concerned. Thank You God for Your grace, Your love, and Your mercy. In the name of Jesus Christ Your Son, I pray, Amen.

SELF-REFLECTION

Are my beliefs and my actions about abortion and sex in line with God's will?

Have I ever encouraged someone to have an abortion or given someone advice about sex that was not in line with God's will?

FOR PARENTS

What am I teaching my child or children about God's will where abortions and sex is concerned?

QUIET TIME WITH GOD

Suggested scripture reading: **Ephesians 4:22–24**

What is God saying to me in this scripture?

_____

_____

6

Deliverance from Detestable Ways

"When you enter the land the Lord your God is giving you, do not learn to imitate the detestable ways of the nations there. Let no one be found among you who sacrifices his son or daughter in the fire, who practices divination or sorcery, interprets omens, engages in witchcraft or cast spells, or who is a medium or spiritualist or who consults the dead. Anyone who does these is detestable to the Lord; because of these same detestable practices the Lord your God will drive out those nations before you."
—Deuteronomy 18:9–12 (NIV)

According to the above scripture, there was a time in my life when I was detestable to the Lord! Defining a few words will help explain why I say this:

Detestable: Offensive behavior.

Offensive: Causing displeasure.

Divination: The act of foreseeing the future or foretelling the unknown, especially by signs and omens.

The word "divination" should not be confused with the word prophecy. Prophecy is not the foretelling of the future based on signs and omens, like divination; rather, it is a divine revelation about the future and is a gift from God, which we should all eagerly desire to have.

"Pursue love, and desire spiritual gifts,
but especially that you may prophesy."
—1 Corinthians 14:1 NKJV)

Sorcery: The use of power gained from the assistance or control of evil spirits.

Witchcraft: The use of sorcery or magic; communication with the devil or a familiar (a familiar is the spirit of a dead person invoked by a medium to advise or prophesy).

Omen: A sign of what is to happen; an object or event that is believed to mean good or bad luck.

Horoscopes: A diagram of the relative positions of planets and signs of the zodiac at a specific time (as at one's birth), for use by astrologers in inferring an individual's character and personality traits and in foretelling events of their life.

Astrology: The divination of the supposed influences of the stars and planets on human affairs and terrestrial events by their positions and aspects.

Medium: An individual held to be a channel of communication between the earthly world and a world of spirits.

Psychic: A person apparently sensitive to nonphysical forces; a medium.

Necromancy: Conjuration of the spirits of the dead for purposes of magically revealing the future or influencing the course of events.

Devil: The main title for the fallen angelic being who is the supreme enemy of God and humankind; a deceiver. Also known as Satan.

Although I was raised to believe in God and His Son Jesus Christ, I was also raised on the interpretations of omens. For example, as 1 Timothy 4:7 (NIV) says, "Have nothing to do with godless myths and old wives' tales, rather train yourself to be godly."

Old wives' tales are defined as a foolish, silly, superstitious belief. Superstitious beliefs are based on something believed to mean good or bad luck; in other words, an omen.

As far back as I can remember, my grandmother and mother practiced superstitious beliefs (my mother more so than my grandmother). One belief in particular that my mother practiced faithfully is what I call the "New Year Superstition Tradition," specifically that having Christmas decorations up on New Year's Day was bad luck. Therefore, all the decorations had to come down before the New Year came in. Ironing or washing clothes on New Year's Day was also considered bad luck.

My mom would hide the iron and unplug the washing machine from New Year's Eve until the day after New Year's Day. If I had something that would need to be clean and ironed during those days, I had to make sure it was done before New

Year's Eve. Additionally, any female who did not live in the house was not allowed to enter on New Year's Day. Having Christmas gifts that had not been unwrapped by New Year's Day; yes, that too was considered to be bad luck.

Therefore, any Christmas gifts we had for other people had to be distributed before New Year's Day. If for some reason we had not gotten around to delivering those gifts, or the person(s) had not come by to get them, then they had to be unwrapped and given to the individuals at a later date, still unwrapped!

Now, on the flipside of all this. On New Year's Day, any male visitor who did not live in the house would have to walk through every room of the house, to represent good luck. Then for dinner, we had to eat black-eyed peas and some type of greens (usually collards or turnips), which represented good luck and prosperity. As a result of these good luck/bad luck beliefs, I literally saw my mother's anxiety level escalate during the holiday season in such a way that really sapped the season of joyousness. A time that should have been about celebrating the birth of Jesus Christ had instead become a time of fear and tension, and talk of celebrating the twelve days of Christmas was not even up for discussion. I even recall a time when I carried around a rabbit's foot for good luck. The truth is, good luck; bad luck; and other superstitious beliefs, old wives' tales, omens, and so on take us further from God and produce fear. This type of fear is not from God.

> *"For God has not given us a*
> *spirit of fear, but of power and of*
> *love and of a sound mind."*
> *—2 Timothy 1:7 (NKJV)*

Reflecting back on that time in my life, I finally came to the realization that Satan had a grip not only on my own life but also on that of my mother. God tells us in His word, "My people are destroyed for lack of knowledge" Hosea 4:6 (NKJV).

I recall my mother telling me that God could not be everywhere; that's why He created mothers. I have even seen the same statement in several books; however, it is not true. God is omnipresent, meaning that He is present everywhere at the same time.

"Where can I go from your Spirit?
Where can I flee from your presence? If I
go up to the heavens, you are there; if I make
my bed in the depths, you are there. If I rise on the
wings of the dawn, if I settle on the far side
of the sea, even there your hand will guide me,
your right hand will hold me fast."
—Psalm 139:7–10 (NIV)

GOD is everywhere.

He sees everything we do, and we are accountable to Him!

"Nothing in all creation is hidden
from God. Everything is naked and
exposed before His eyes, and He is the one
to whom we are accountable."
—Hebrews 4:13 (NLT)

Growing up with these kinds of beliefs was an open door for the Devil to continue entering into my life, for instance, through certain television shows. When I was a little girl, one of my favorite TV shows was based on the use of magical powers. I was so intrigued by how someone could make things happen just by doing a few gestures. I even found myself trying to do the same, especially when I was told to clean up my room; of course, it never worked! I watched this show until I was fourteen years old, when it went off the air. By then, of course, I knew that the show was fictitious. What I didn't realize at the time, however, was that as innocent as the show seemed, the door that the Devil had opened was now opening wider and wider.

In my high school history class, we often had to bring in articles about current events, mainly from the newspaper. One section in the newspaper really caught my attention: the daily horoscope. Every morning before school, after I had bathed and dressed, and while waiting for my grandmother to prepare breakfast, I would get the newspaper and quickly turn to the horoscopes to see what mine said for the day. I did this faithfully every day. I also had several T-shirts and other paraphernalia advertising astrology; I even believed that I should only date people who were compatible to my zodiac sign.

However, I did at times date guys who were

not compatible with my sign, and whenever we had some sort of disagreement or conflict in our relationship, I would be quick to blame our difficulties on our zodiac incompatibility. When looking back on those days and my way of thinking, I have often wondered how many of the guys who tried to date me back then were sent by God, and whom I turned away or broke up with because, according to my way of thinking at the time, we were incompatible.

For years, I continued believing in horoscopes and zodiac signs, and watching TV shows featuring people with magical powers. One particular show was about three women who were considered to be "Good Witches" as they used their powers for good. This show began a few months after my mother had passed, and it reminded me of something my mother had once told me: "There is black magic, and there is white magic." The explanation she gave was as follows: "Black magic is evil and should never be used, but white magic is used to help people and is okay to do." Thus, the show reminded me of my mother's explanation of the difference between black magic and white magic. Needless to say, I felt a connection to my mother through this show. It was this show that led me to start reading books on spells and white magic, in addition to books on astrology, zodiac signs, and so on.

Eventually, with the help of one of my aunts, I even began seeking guidance from psychics/mediums. Without realizing it, I was being drawn further and further away from God. One day, I purchased a Ouija Board. A few of my cousins and I got together and decided to practice necromancy with it. I don't remember exactly whom we were trying to talk to or the questions we were trying to get answers to. However, I do remember a group of folding chairs that were stacked up against the wall, which all of a sudden fell over as if someone had pushed them. Well, that did it for me! I jumped up from the table and did not want to continue playing with the Ouija Board, nor did I want to keep the board. I wanted it out of the house, and I was very serious about that. I recall my cousin taking it; I told him to get rid of it, although I am not sure that he did. To be honest, at the time I really didn't care what he did with it. I just wanted it gone! I was believing in things that are detestable to God. It wasn't too long after this that I had the divine encounter described in Chapter 1.

I began drawing closer to God, and He was drawing closer to me; and yes, Satan still had a grip on me. I was battling between good and evil. I was in a spiritual warfare; nobody really understood what I was going through, and I didn't really know how to explain it at the time. It got to the point where my family thought I was having a mental breakdown. I was even evaluated by doctors, only for them to find nothing wrong with me. There were times when I felt all alone, but yet, I knew that I wasn't. God has always been there for me, and has promised to "never leave me nor forsake me" (scripture reference Joshua 1:5). God has always had His hand on me; even in my mother's womb, He protected me.

My mother told me that she was in an electrical explosion during her ninth month of pregnancy with me. She was blown completely out of the house yet had only a few splinters as a result. I was born a few weeks before her due date. Even then, the Devil was trying to destroy me, but God had other plans for me.

"For I know the plans I have for you,"
declares the LORD, *"plans to prosper*
you and not to harm you, plans to give
you hope and a future."
—Jeremiah 29:11 (NIV)

One of God's plans for me was for me to not be under Satan's control any longer. I knew that I had to repent from these detestable ways, but unlike with the candy molds and everything else, because of Satan's strong grip on me at that time, repentance in this case meant more than just my turning from these detestable ways.

"And he said unto them,
This kind can come forth by nothing,
but by prayer and fasting."
—Mark 9:29 (KJV)

There are some translations of the Bible that leave out the word "fasting," but I have learned that both fasting and praying together are important, and they were definitely needed in my case. I prayed, asking God what kind of fast He would have me do. God instructed me on the kind of fast that He wanted me to do and how long I was to do it. As I did this fast along with much prayer, Satan's grip on me was loosening day by day, and I was being filled with more of the Holy Spirit each day; I trusted God to show me everything that I needed to get rid of and guide me in doing so. I began with all of my T-shirts advertising astrology and zodiac signs. I took the T-shirts, along with other clothing that God showed me to get rid of, and cut them into pieces as small as I could and tied them up in a bag. Having learned about spiritual warfare at this point, I found it so interesting that, as a Christian family, we had so many things in our home that were detestable to God.

For example, when I was in my early twenties, my mother and I had taken a ceramic class together. I had made an elephant flower vase, and she had made a golden Buddha. She placed the Buddha on the table in the foyer and would often rub its belly for good luck, encouraging me to do the same; I did so a few times, but somehow, it didn't feel right (I now know why). Although this Buddha gave me the sentimental memory of my mother and I taking the class together, God revealed to me in the following three scriptures that this statue was something that I could not keep.

"Do not make idols or set up an image
or a sacred stone for yourselves, and do not
place a carved stone in your land to bow down
before it. I am the LORD your God."
—Leviticus 26:1 (NIV)

"But their idols are silver and gold,
made by human hands."
—Psalm 115:4 (NIV)

"Do not bow down before their gods or
worship them or follow their practices.
You must demolish them and break their
sacred stones to pieces."
—Exodus 23:24 (NIV)

I did exactly that. I broke the Buddha statue into pieces and threw it away. Afterward, I gathered all the books I had that were associated with these detestable ways, along with the bag of cut up clothes, and had a Book-B-Que! I literally burned them all up along with the grip that the devil had on me. The demon that had tormented me, making my family believe I was having a mental breakdown, finally came out of me. Satan's power over me was finally broken. God delivered me from the power of Satan!

"He has delivered us from the power of darkness and conveyed us into the kingdom of the Son of His love."
—Colossians 1:13 (NKJV)

My Prayer

*Gracious and Merciful Father, thank you
God, that even when I was not seeking you
for guidance in my life, and I had turned to
detestable ways, You God had your hand on
me; You never left my side, and You never
stopped loving me. Thank you, Father God, for
delivering me from these detestable ways.
In the name of Jesus, I pray, Amen.*

SELF-REFLECTION

Are any of my ways detestable to the Lord?

When I wear T–shirts, what am I advertising?

FOR PARENTS

Are any of the TV shows, movies, or video
games that my child/children watch, or play
with, leading them to be detestable to the Lord?

QUIET TIME WITH GOD

Suggested scripture reading: **Psalm 139:23–24**

What is God saying to me in this scripture?

_____

_____

7

The Importance of Prayer

"Pray without ceasing."
—1 Thessalonians 5:17 (NKJV)

Prayer is simply talking to God. To "pray without ceasing," as the above scripture says, means to be constantly in communication with God. I learned the importance of prayer at an early age. I was eight years old. My mother was in the hospital, which was at that time a Catholic hospital. I was told that she was diagnosed with locked bowels (meaning she was unable to have a bowel movement). I was also told that while surgery was an option, there was no guarantee that it would work, and if she did have the surgery, she might not survive. The next day, I was able to go see her. Children under twelve were not allowed in patients' rooms, but a nun made an exception and walked me up to my mother's room. While I was in the room with her, the doctor came in. He basically said the same thing that I had been told about her diagnosis but he also said that "The best thing would be for her to have a bowel movement on her own, so that she would not have to have surgery." In other words, if she did not have a bowel movement soon, my dad was going to have to make a decision about her having surgery in a few days.

After learning this news, I kept my mother lifted up in prayer. At night, before I went to bed, I would say my prayers, asking God to heal my mother so she wouldn't have to have surgery. A few days went by, and she had not had a bowel movement. My dad had to make a decision. He chose for her to have surgery. Still, I prayed. The day for her surgery came, and again the nun walked me up to her room. Upon entering my mom's room, I ran over to her, and gave her a kiss and a big hug. With tears in my eyes, I said to her, "I love you mommy, I'm praying for you." She replied, "I love you a bushel and a peck and a hug around the neck" (this was a phrase that she often said to me). A few minutes later, the transporters came to take her to the operating room. As I stood back and watched them lift her off the bed to put her on the stretcher, I was still praying, though not aloud. As they wheeled her out of the room, I was still praying, "God heal my mommy, please don't let her have to have surgery, please help her use the bathroom, God."

For a moment I was just standing there saying this prayer over and over in my head. Before we could gather our belongings and leave the room, they were bringing her back in. I could hear my dad saying, "What's wrong, what happened?" The transporter said, "Her surgery has been cancelled. She had a bowel movement on the way to the operating room, and the doctor has cancelled her surgery." God answered my prayer! I was a happy little girl. As soon as she was back in bed, with tears of joy running down my face, I ran over to give her a big hug. I was so happy! God had healed my mother, and she was going to be alright!

Since then, many of my prayers have been answered; many others have been unanswered. As God began transforming my life, I began to understand just what the importance of prayer really is. It's more than just asking God for something; it's developing a relationship with Him.

Like any relationship, that means spending time with God, and being in constant communication with Him.

Reflecting back on my early schooldays, I recall how we were in constant communication with God even at school. In the morning before class, a prayer was said, and before dismissal, prayer was said again. Sometimes the teacher said the prayer, sometimes a student said it. Then, in between, we had a Bible class just like any other class. We had to learn and memorize scriptures, and apply them to our life. Knowing what I know now about prayer, and what I have experienced, I truly believe that our constant communication with God helped us to have peace in our school. I have come to learn that God changes things when we pray.

"If my people, which are called by my name, shall humble themselves, and pray, and seek my face, and turn from their wicked ways; then will I hear from heaven, and will forgive their sin, and will heal their land."
—2 Chronicles 7:14 (KJV)

My Prayer

Heavenly Father, thank you that I don't have to talk to several people to reach You, but rather, I have a direct line to You without even being put on hold! I can come and talk to You anytime, about anything, no matter where I am, and You are never too busy to listen. Your ears are attentive to my prayer. Thank You Father that as I pray according to Your will, my prayers are answered. In the mighty name of Your Son Jesus I pray, Amen.

SELF-REFLECTION

What kind of relationship do I have with God?

Do I try to solve my own problems instead of seeking God for guidance?

FOR PARENTS

Is my prayer life setting a good example for my child/children to know how to pray?

QUIET TIME WITH GOD

Suggested scripture reading: **Philippians 4:6–7**

What is God saying to me in this scripture?

_____

_____

Conclusion

*"The Lord is not slack concerning His promise, as
some count slackness, but is longsuffering toward
us, not willing that any should perish but that all
should come to repentance."*
—2 Peter 3:9 (NKJV)

The Common English Bible
(CEB) says it this way:
*"The Lord isn't slow to keep his promise, as some
think of slowness, but he is patient toward you, not
wanting anyone to perish but all to change their
hearts and lives."*

The Contemporary English Version
(CEV) says it yet this way:
*"The Lord isn't slow about keeping
his promises, as some people think*

69

he is. In fact, God is patient, because
he wants everyone to turn from sin
and no one to be lost."

I know for a fact that God is a very patient God because He was patient with me. Accepting Jesus Christ as my Lord and Savior was one of the best choices that I have ever made, for truly there is no other name in which we are saved other than the name of Jesus (Acts 4:11–12), and there is no other way to the Father except through His Son Jesus Christ.

"Jesus said to him, 'I am the way, the
truth, and the life. No one comes to the
Father except through Me.'"
—John 14:6 (NKJV)

I am ever so thankful that God did not treat me as my sins deserved. Instead, God loved me enough to not let me stay in my sinful ways. He delivered me from those things that are not pleasing in His sight. God forgave me for my sins and remembers them no more. Because of what Jesus did for me, God, reconciled me to Himself, putting me in a right relationship with Him, and as a result, I became a new creation in Christ.

> *"Therefore, if anyone is in Christ,*
> *the new creation has come: The old*
> *has gone, the new is here!"*
> —*2 Corinthians 5:17 (NKJV)*

He did all of this so that I might live and have life more abundantly. This does not make me perfect; only Jesus is perfect, I am just a sinner saved by grace. The good news is that what God did for me, He can do for all people, because He created all people. I am a living example that it does not matter what you have done or what sins you have committed, and it definitely doesn't matter what color your skin is. What does matter is having a relationship with God through Christ.

Entering this relationship with God starts with:

1) Accepting Jesus Christ as Lord and Savior. "For if you tell others with your own mouth that Jesus Christ is your Lord, and believe in your own heart that God has raised him

from the dead, you will be saved. For it is by believing in his heart that a man becomes right with God; and with his mouth he tells others of his faith, confirming his salvation" (Romans 10:9–10).

2) Prayer . . . talking to God about everything.
3) Fellowshipping with other believers.
4) Spending quiet time with God daily, studying His word, and listening to what He says through His word: the Bible.

"The whole Bible was given to us by inspiration from God and is useful to teach us what is true and to make us realize what is wrong in our lives; it straightens us out and helps us to do what is right."
—*2 Timothy 3:16 (TLB)*

I'M A WITNESS!

The Lord's Prayer

Our Father which art in heaven,
Hallowed be thy name.
Thy kingdom come.
Thy will be done in earth, as it is in heaven.
Give us this day our daily bread.
And forgive us our debts, as we
forgive our debtors.
And lead us not into temptation,
but deliver us from evil:
For thine is the kingdom, and the
power, and the glory, for ever.
Amen.
—Matthew 6:9–13 (KJV)

P.O. Box 453
Powder Springs, Georgia 30127
www.entegritypublishing.com
info@entegritypublishing.com

www.ingramcontent.com/pod-product-compliance
Lightning Source LLC
Chambersburg PA
CBHW060254150626
46553CB00019BA/2287